hope you enjoy!
Love always,
Auntie Anne
x x x

Albert Einstein
Quotes...
by The Secret Libraries

Paperback EDITION

Vol.9

Find us on:

The Secret Libraries

Published by The Secret Libraries
www.thesecretlibraries.com
Annotation and Artists Background by The Secret Libraries 2016

Paperback:
ISBN-13: 978-1539309161
ISBN-10: 1539309169

Quotes...

This book provides a selected collection of 201 quotes by Albert Einstein.

Albert Einstein

1879-1955

Two things are infinite: the universe and human stupidity; and I'm not sure about the universe.

Science without religion is lame, religion without science is blind.

If you can't explain it simply, you don't understand it well enough.

Logic will get you from A to B. Imagination will take you everywhere.

Insanity: doing the same thing over and over again and expecting different results.

There are only two ways to live your life. One is as though nothing is a miracle. The other is as though everything is a miracle.

Great spirits have always encountered violent opposition from mediocre minds.

Everything should be made as simple as possible, but not simpler.

Reality is merely an illusion, albeit a very persistent one.

I am enough of an artist to draw freely upon my imagination. Imagination is more important than knowledge. Knowledge is limited. Imagination encircles the world.

If you want your children to be intelligent, read them fairy tales. If you want them to be more intelligent, read them more fairy tales.

If you can't explain it to a six year old, you don't understand it yourself.

$$E = mc^2$$

Life is like riding a bicycle. To keep your balance, you must keep moving.

Anyone who has never made a mistake has never tried anything new.

I speak to everyone in the same way, whether he is the garbage man or the president of the university.

When you are courting a nice girl an hour seems like a second. When you sit on a red-hot cinder a second seems like an hour. That's relativity.

Never memorize something that you can look up.

A clever person solves a problem. A wise person avoids it.

A happy man is too satisfied with the present to dwell too much on the future.

If we knew what it was we were doing, it would not be called research, would it?

I have no special talents. I am only passionately curious.

If a cluttered desk is a sign of a cluttered mind, of what, then, is an empty desk a sign?

"

The important thing is to not stop questioning. Curiosity has its own reason for existence. One cannot help but be in awe when he contemplates the mysteries of eternity, of life, of the marvelous structure of reality. It is enough if one tries merely to comprehend a little of this mystery each day.

"

Try not to become a man of success. Rather become a man of value.

A human being is a part of the whole called by us universe, a part limited in time and space. He experiences himself, his thoughts and feeling as something separated from the rest, a kind of optical delusion of his consciousness. This delusion is a kind of prison for us, restricting us to our personal desires and to affection for a few persons nearest to us.

Any fool can know. The point is to understand.

Once you can accept the universe as matter expanding into nothing that is something, wearing stripes with plaid comes easy.

If I were not a physicist, I would probably be a musician. I often think in music. I live my daydreams in music. I see my life in terms of music..

The world as we have created it is a process of our thinking. It cannot be changed without changing our thinking.

I know not with what weapons World War III will be fought, but World War IV will be fought with sticks and stones.

You never fail until you stop trying.

Whether you can observe a thing or not depends on the theory which you use. It is the theory which decides what can be observed.

Gravitation is not responsible for people falling in love.

The most beautiful experience we can have is the mysterious. It is the fundamental emotion that stands at the cradle of true art and true science.

It is not that I'm so smart. But I stay with the questions much longer.

Creativity is intelligence having fun.

The measure of intelligence is the ability to change.

The world is a dangerous place to live, not because of the people who are evil, but because of the people who don't do anything about it.

If A is a success in life, then A equals x plus y plus z. Work is x; y is play; and z is keeping your mouth shut.

Black holes are where God divided by zero.

The best way to cheer yourself is to cheer somebody else up.

When you trip over love, it is easy to get up. But when you fall in love, it is impossible to stand again.

What is right is not always popular and what is popular is not always right.

The pursuit of truth and beauty is a sphere of activity in which we are permitted to remain children all our lives.

I take it to be true that pure thought can grasp the real, as the ancients had dreamed.

Whoever is careless with the truth in small matters cannot be trusted with important matters.

Men marry women with the hope they will never change. Women marry men with the hope they will change. Invariably they are both disappointed.

Peace cannot be kept by force; it can only be achieved by understanding.

A question that sometimes drives me hazy: am I or are the others crazy?

We dance for laughter, we dance for tears, we dance for madness, we dance for fears, we dance for hopes, we dance for screams, we are the dancers, we create the dreams.

Imagination is everything. It is the preview of life's coming attractions.

If the facts don't fit the theory, change the facts.

The important thing is not to stop questioning.
Curiosity has its own reason for existing.

The woman who follows the crowd will usually go no further than the crowd. The woman who walks alone is likely to find herself in places no one has ever been before.

"

I must be willing to give up what I am in order to become what I will be.

"

Love is a better master than duty.

Time is an illusion.

It would be possible to describe everything scientifically, but it would make no sense; it would be without meaning, as if you described a Beethoven symphony as a variation of wave pressure.

Blind belief in authority is the greatest enemy of truth.

Science can flourish only in an atmosphere of free speech.

We all know that light travels faster than sound. That's why certain people appear bright until you hear them speak.

I'd rather be an optimist and a fool than a pessimist and right.

I never made one of my discoveries through the process of rational thinking.

Genius is 1% talent and 99% percent hard work...

Nothing happens until something moves.

Once we accept our limits, we go beyond them.

Only a life lived for others is a life worthwhile.

A ship is always safe at the shore - but that is NOT what it is built for.

Few are those who see with their own eyes and feel with their own hearts.

If you want to live a happy life, tie it to a goal, not to people or things.

God does not play dice with the universe.

Imagination is the highest form of research.

However rare true love may be, it is less so than true friendship.

Our task must be to free ourselves... by widening our circle of compassion to embrace all living creatures and the whole of nature and its beauty.

I never think of the future - it comes soon enough.

The most incomprehensible thing about the world is that it is at all comprehensible.

Weakness of attitude becomes weakness of character.

What a sad era when it is easier to smash an atom than a prejudice.

than a prejudice.

Only those who attempt the absurd can achieve the impossible.

You can never solve a problem on the level on which it was created.

I live in that solitude which is painful in youth, but delicious in the years of maturity.

Look deep into nature, and then you will understand everything better.

Student: Dr. Einstein, Aren't these the same questions as last year's [physics] final exam?

Dr. Einstein: Yes; But this year the answers are different.

The hardest thing in the world to understand is the income tax.

Wisdom is not a product of schooling but of the lifelong attempt to acquire it.

You cannot simultaneously prevent and prepare for war.

I love Humanity but I hate humans.

From the standpoint of daily life, however, there is one thing we do know: that we are here for the sake of each other - above all for those upon whose smile and well-being our own happiness depends, and also for the countless unknown souls with whose fate we are connected by a bond of sympathy. Many times a day I realize how much my own outer and inner life is built upon the labors of my fellow men, both living and dead, and how earnestly I must exert myself in order to give in return as much as I have received.

Imagination is more important than knowledge. For knowledge is limited to all we now know and understand, while imagination embraces the entire world, and all there ever will be to know and understand.

If people are good only because they fear punishment, and hope for reward, then we are a sorry lot indeed.

Common sense is the collection of prejudices acquired by age eighteen.

A true genius admits that he/she knows nothing.

If there is any religion that could respond to the needs of modern science, it would be Buddhism.

If I had an hour to solve a problem I'd spend 55 minutes thinking about the problem and 5 minutes thinking about solutions.

The only thing that you absolutely have to know, is the location of the library.

Few people are capable of expressing with equanimity opinions which differ from the prejudices of their social enviroment. Most people are incapable of forming such opinions.

I cannot imagine a God who rewards and punishes the objects of his creation, whose purposes are modeled after our own -- a God, in short, who is but a reflection of human frailty. Neither can I believe that the individual survives the death of his body, although feeble souls harbor such thoughts through fear or ridiculous egotisms.

I believe in intuitions and inspirations...I sometimes FEEL that I am right. I do not KNOW that I am.

The only real valuable thing is intuition.

Life is a preparation for the future; and the best preparation for the future is to live as if there were none.

My religion consists of a humble admiration of the illimitable superior spirit who reveals himself in the slight details we are able to perceive with our frail and feeble mind.

If at first the idea is not absurd, then there is no hope for it.

When I examine myself and my methods of thought, I come to the conclusion that the gift of fantasy has meant more to me than any talent for abstract, positive thinking.

When the solution is simple, God is answering.

A person starts to live when he can live outside himself.

I want to know God's thoughts - the rest are mere details.

The tragedy of life is what dies inside a man while he lives.

Laws alone can not secure freedom of expression; in order that every man present his views without penalty there must be spirit of tolerance in the entire population.

One thing I have learned in a long life: that all our science, measured against reality, is primitive and childlike -- and yet it is the most precious thing we have.

The only thing that interferes with my learning is my education.

The Revolution introduced me to art, and in turn, art introduced me to the Revolution!

Somebody who only reads newspapers and at best books of contemporary authors looks to me like an extremely near-sighted person who scorns eyeglasses. He is completely dependent on the prejudices and fashions of his times, since he never gets to see or hear anything else.

Intellectual growth should commence at birth and cease only at death.

We know from daily life that we exist for other people first of all, for whose smiles and well-being our own happiness depends.

Your question is the most difficult in the world. It is not a question I can answer simply with yes or no. I am not an Atheist. I do not know if I can define myself as a Pantheist. The problem involved is too vast for our limited minds

Even on the most solemn occasions I got away without wearing socks and hid that lack of civilization in high boots.

The ideals which have always shone before me and filled me with joy are goodness, beauty, and truth.

He who joyfully marches to music rank and file has already earned my contempt. He has been given a large brain by mistake, since for him the spinal cord would surely suffice. This disgrace to civilization should be done away with at once. Heroism at command, senseless brutality, deplorable love-of-country stance and all the loathsome nonsense that goes by the name of patriotism, how violently I hate all this, how despicable and ignoble war is.

The word 'God' is for me nothing more than the expression and product of human weaknesses, the Bible a collection of honorable, but still primitive legends which are nevertheless pretty childish. No interpretation, no matter how subtle, can (for me) change this.

God is subtle but he is not malicious.

No, this trick won't work... How on earth are you ever going to explain in terms of chemistry and physics so important a biological phenomenon as first love?

The true sign of intelligence is not knowledge but imagination.

A man should look for what is, and not for what he thinks should be.

Information is not knowledge.

Energy cannot be created or destroyed, it can only be changed from one form to another.

The only sure way to avoid making mistakes is to have no new ideas.

Possessions, outward success, publicity, luxury - to me these have always been contemptible. I believe that a simple and unassuming manner of life is best for everyone, best for both the body and the mind.

Dancers are the athletes of God.

It is the supreme art of the teacher to awaken joy in creative expression and knowledge.

Everything is determined, the beginning as well as the end, by forces over which we have no control. It is determined for the insect, as well as for the star. Human beings, vegetables, or cosmic dust, we all dance to a mysterious tune, intoned in the distance by an invisible piper.

It is, in fact, nothing short of a miracle that the modern methods of instruction have not yet entirely strangled the holy curiosity of inquiry; for this delicate little plant, aside from stimulation, stands mainly in need of freedom. Without this it goes to wrack and ruin without fail.

All religions, arts and sciences are branches of the same tree. All these aspirations are directed toward ennobling man's life, lifting it from the sphere of mere physical existence and leading the individual towards freedom.

The only escape from the miseries of life are music and cats...

Student is not a container you have to fill but a torch you have to light up.

We can not solve our problems with the same level of thinking that created them.

I never teach my pupils, I only attempt to provide the conditions in which they can learn.

You have to learn the rules of the game. And then you have to play better than anyone else.

If I were to remain silent, I'd be guilty of complicity.

The insight into the mystery of life, coupled though it be with fear, has also given rise to religion. To know what is impenetrable to us really exists, manifesting itself as the highest wisdom and the most radiant beauty, which our dull faculties can comprehend only in their most primitive forms—this knowledge, this feeling is at the center of true religiousness.

As far as the laws of mathematics refer to reality, they are not certain; and as far as they are certain, they do not refer to reality.

I thought of that while riding my bicycle.

Before God we are all equally wise - and equally foolish.

The only source of knowledge is experience.

Play is the highest form of research.

Einstein was once asked how many feet are in a mile. Einstein's reply was "I don't know, why should I fill my brain with facts I can find in two minutes in any standard reference book?

Past is dead

Future is uncertain;
Present is all you have,
So eat, drink and live merry.

At least once a day, allow yourself the freedom to think and dream for yourself.

The true value of a human being can be found in the degree to which he has attained liberation from the self.

Force always attracts men of low morality.

Three great forces rule the world: stupidity, fear and greed.

It seems to me that the idea of a personal God is an anthropological concept which I cannot take seriously. I also cannot imagine some will or goal outside the human sphere... Science has been charged with undermining morality, but the charge is unjust. A man's ethical behavior should be based effectually on sympathy, education, and social ties and needs; no religious basis is necessary. Man would indeed be in a poor way if he had to be restrained by fear of punishment and hope of reward after death.

If my theory of relativity is proven successful, Germany will claim me as a German and France will declare me a citizen of the world. Should my theory prove untrue, France will say that I am a German, and Germany will declare that I am a Jew.

A foolish faith in authority is the worst enemy of truth.

My passionate sense of social justice and social responsibility has always contrasted oddly with my pronounced lack of need for direct contact with other human beings and human communities. I am truly a 'lone traveler' and have never belonged to my country, my home, my friends, or even my immediate family, with my whole heart; in the face of all these ties, I have never lost a sense of distance and a need for solitude....

An empty stomach is not a good political adviser.

We experience ourselves our thoughts and feelings as something separate from the rest. A kind of optical delusion of consciousness. This delusion is a kind of prison for us, restricting us to our personal desires and to affection for a few persons nearest to us.

Solitude is painful when one is young, but delightful when one is more mature.

What really interests me is whether God had any choice in the creation of the World.

A table, a chair, a bowl of fruit and a violin; what else does a man need to be happy?

The human spirit must prevail over technology.

Teaching should be such that what is offered is perceived as a valuable gift and not as hard duty. Never regard study as duty but as the enviable opportunity to learn to know the liberating influence of beauty in the realm of the spirit for your own personal joy and to the profit of the community to which your later work belongs.

Compound interest is the eighth wonder of the world. He who understands it, earns it ... he who doesn't ... pays it.

Science is international but its success is based on institutions, which are owned by nations. If therefore, we wish to promote culture we have to combine and to organize institutions with our own power and means.

No amount of experimentation can ever prove me right; a single experiment can prove me wrong.

I don't try to imagine a personal God; it suffices to stand in awe at the structure of the world, insofar as it allows our inadequate senses to appreciate it.

Learning is experience. Everything else is just information.

If most of us are ashamed of shabby clothes and shoddy furniture let us be more ashamed of shabby ideas and shoddy philosophies.... It would be a sad situation if the wrapper were better than the meat wrapped inside it.

Although I am a typical loner in my daily life, my awareness of belonging to the invisible community of those who strive for truth, beauty, and justice has prevented me from feelings of isolation.

All generalizations are false, including this one.

We are in the position of a little child entering a huge library, whose walls are covered to the ceiling with books in many different languages. The child knows that someone must have written those books. It does not know who or how. It does not understand the the languages in which they are written. The child notes a definite plan in the arrangement of the books, a mysterious order, which it does not comprehend but only dimly suspects.

You see, wire telegraph is a kind of a very, very long cat. You pull his tail in New York and his head is meowing in Los Angeles. Do you understand this? And radio operates exactly the same way: you send signals here, they receive them there. The only difference is that there is no cat.

Excellence is doing a common thing in an uncommon way.

Small is the number of them that see with their own eyes and feel with their own hearts.

"

One cannot alter a condition with the same mind set that created it in the first place.

"

How I wish that somewhere there existed an island for those who are wise and of good will.

He to whom this emotion is a stranger, who can no longer pause to wonder and stand rapt in awe, is as good as dead: his eyes are closed.

The more I learn, the more I realize how much I don't know.

It gives me great pleasure indeed to see the stubbornness of an incorrigible nonconformist warmly acclaimed.

Never do anything against conscience, even if the state demands it.

Everything that is really great and inspiring is created by the individual who can labor in freedom.

Nothing will benefit human health and increase the chances for survival of life on Earth as much as the evolution to a vegetarian diet.

Strange is our situation here on Earth. Each of us comes for a short visit, not knowing why, yet sometimes seeming to divine a purpose. From the standpoint of daily life, however, there is one thing we do know: that man is here for the sake of other men - above all for those upon whose smiles and well-being our own happiness depends.

If you don't have time to do it right, when will you have time to do it over?

The bigotry of the nonbeliever is for me nearly as funny as the bigotry of the believer.

Everyone must become their own person, however frightful that may be.

It occurred to me by intuition, and music was the driving force behind that intuition. My discovery was the result of musical perception.

Our separation from each other is an optical illusion.

Always do what's right; this will gratify some and astonish the rest.

It is my conviction that killing under the cloak of war is nothing but an act of murder.

Intelligence is not the ability to store information, but to know where to find it.

I believe that Gandhi's views were the most enlightened of all the political men in our time. We should strive to do things in his spirit: not to use violence in fighting for our cause, but by non-participation in anything you believe is evil.

Older men start wars, but younger men fight them.

To dwell on the things that depress or anger us does not help in overcoming them. One must knock them down alone.

Out of clutter, find simplicity. From discord, find harmony. In the middle of difficulty lies opportunity.

Truth is what stands the test of experience.

Generations to come, it may well be, will scarce believe that such a man as this one ever in flesh and blood walked upon this Earth.

What I see in Nature is a magnificent structure that we can comprehend only very imperfectly, and that must fill a thinking person with a feeling of humility. This is a genuinely religious feeling that has nothing to do with mysticism.

Now he has departed from this strange world a little ahead of me. That means nothing. People like us, who believe in physics, know that the distinction between past, present, and future is only a stubbornly persistent illusion.

A society's competitive advantage will come not from how well its schools teach the multiplication and periodic tables, but from how well they stimulate imagination and creativity.

To punish me for my contempt for authority, fate made me an authority myself.

Albert Einstein

1879–1955

References & Further Reading
Works from Albert Einstein

Scientific career
Special relativity
General relativity
Mass–energy equivalence (E=MC2)
Photoelectric effect
Einstein solid
Equivalence principle
Einstein field equations
Einstein radius
Einstein relation (kinetic theory)
Cosmological constant
Einstein–Cartan theory
Einstein–Infeld–Hoffmann equations
Einstein–de Haas effect
EPR paradox
Bose–Einstein condensate
Bose–Einstein statistics
Bose–Einstein correlations
Bohr–Einstein debates
Brownian motion
Teleparallelism

Works:
Annus Mirabilis papers (1905)
"Investigations on the Theory of Brownian Movement" (1905)
Relativity: The Special and the General Theory (1916)
The World as I See It (1949)
"Why Socialism?" (1949)
Russell–Einstein Manifesto (1955)

Albert Einstein

Quotes...

Receive a Kindle Edition in the series for FREE...

Sign up at
www.theSECREtlibraries.com

Find us on:

The Secret Libraries

Published by The Secret Libraries
www.thesecretlibraries.com
Annotation and Artists Background by The Secret Libraries 2016

Paperback:
ISBN-13: 978-1539309161
ISBN-10: 1539309169

For more information please find us at:

www.theSeCret libraries.com

Thank you for your purchase.